Neat and Clean

Written by
Jill Atkins

Illustrated by
Alex Patrick

Ray Neat was neat. Kay Clean was clean.

They were proud to be neat and clean.

One day, the sun was hot and there were no clouds.

"Let us go out," said Ray Neat.

"Oh yes," said Kay Clean. "Shall we go to the farm?"

"I like going there," said Ray. "It will be a real treat."

They got their clean boots and their neat coats.

Ray tied a clean scarf around his neck.

Kay tied a neat bonnet under her chin.

Then they set off.

Soon they spied a lad with red hair.

Jay was sitting on a wooden seat.

"We are going to the farm," said Kay Clean.

"Oh, no," said the lad. "Do not go that way. There is a lot of mud across there. It is thick clay."

"Oh," said Ray Neat. "Well, I must say that it will not matter. We have long boots on."

So off they went.

Soon they found that the lad was right. The mud was brown and wet. It was thick clay.

Then Ray Neat found that his boot was stuck in a mound of clay.

"Oh no!" he cried. "I have lost a boot in a mound of clay! I will have to hop."

Then Kay Clean fell down flat on her back.

"Oh no!" she cried. "My bonnet is dripping and my coat is no longer clean."

On they went, plodding and hopping and hopping and plodding.

At the farm, they met Fay.

"Do not go that way," Fay said, pointing down the hill. "The hay has been harvested. You may trip and land in it."

But Ray Neat and Kay Clean went on, hopping and plodding down the hill into the hay.

Soon they found that Fay was right.

They plodded along in the hay, and the hay stuck to the clay on their boots and coats.

Kay stood looking at Ray.

"Oh, you are a sight!" she cried. "And I have not had so much fun in years."

"You look a treat, too," cried Ray. "This outing is such a thrill."

"I am no longer Kay Clean," said Kay.

"And I am no longer Ray Neat," said Ray.

"Let us stay on this farm. We will help the farmer."

And so they did!